What Binds Us

poems by

Cheryl Wilder

Finishing Line Press
Georgetown, Kentucky

What Binds Us

for Mom
1948 - 2016

ACKNOWLEDGMENTS

The author gratefully acknowledges the editors of the publications, in which
some of the poems first appeared, a few in slightly different form.

Literary Mama: "In Parentheses"
Cream City Review: "What Binds Us"
Connotation Press: "Foundation," "Where I Don't Live"
Strong Verse: "Spring Cleaning in Winter," "Disconnected"

Many thanks to Mark Cox, Richard Jackson, Robin Behn, Nancy Eimers,
Lavonne Adams, Thomas Lux, and Ligon Flynn—mentors who believed in my
work and helped shape the artist I am today. To all my family and friends for
their unending support and encouragement, it means the world having you in
my corner. I honestly couldn't thank you enough. And to my husband, my shelter
from the storm, thank you always.

If it wasn't for Claire Guyton and Suzanne Farrell Smith's friendship, smarts, and
enthusiasm there's no doubt this book would still be sitting on my hard drive.
Many thanks to you both and Karin Wiberg for helping with the details. For
everyone at Finishing Line Press, I am inspired by the work you do and grateful
that you took this collection under your wing.

Publisher: Leah Maines
Editor: Christen Kincaid
Cover Design: Elizabeth Maines McCleavy
Author Photo: Elizabeth Galecke
Cover Art: Connie L. Stewart

Printed in the USA on acid-free paper.
Order online: www.finishinglinepress.com
also available on amazon.com

Author inquiries and mail orders:
Finishing Line Press
PO Box 1626
Georgetown, Kentucky 40324
USA

Table of Contents

What Binds Us

When my grandmother and mother are together they get asked if they are twins
                  my mom has to hear how she's the younger, uglier one.
        I don't think grandmother means to hurt her

but since she doesn't know how to speak of my
                grandfather dying, she calls mom
      a murderer for putting a sick cat to sleep.

He isn't my mom's dad, that grandfather died years ago
                talking of how his third wife was karma
      for the treatment of his first wife,

my grandmother, who thanks me for thinking of her
                when I send school pictures of my son. My grandmother
      whose children were stolen from her, who allowed them to believe

she didn't want them, which is what their father said, my grandfather,
                who died
      telling no one. My mom,

who looks more aged than her mother, never
                asked any questions, her sister asked so many
      she shot herself.

The cat, who was sick, my mom replaced with a dog
                so something would look forward to her
      coming home.

As If We Know

Yellow crusted Q-tips
and coiled maxi pads are piled
inches from a friend's blushed face. I sit

with my feet in the sink watching
her French manicure grip the toilet
as if lifting to sip Miso soup. She's throwing-up oysters

and doesn't want to hear that, like mollusks,
we're a filtration system—at over twenty feet long
our intestines should flow like Roman aqueducts, yet they lie

kinked and twisted like forgotten hoses in tall grass.
When I was twenty I stopped eating meat
the pecking pain forced me

into the fetal position. But for some it's milk
that congests their insides; abuse,
peanuts, loneliness, raw broccoli, legumes,

abandonment. My father stopped talking
to me that year. Guilt, wheat, heartache,
shame, shellfish—fears digest as if we know

what is right or that right even exists.

Flood

The river creeps underneath the deck.
The storm door speaks to wind
that sneaks inside, moves his stagnant
razor shavings, my nightmares of leaving.
I wear my dead grandmother's nightgown
and my son suckles at my breast, his tiny fingers
curled around the embroidered rose neckline.
A roof floats by. I know if I turn my head
I will see his father lying on the couch, beaten
by the day's arrival, comforted in the blanket of rain
that allows him to stay inside. I have my own need
to stay. Time is but an illusion of movement forward.
In the same moment the little warm breath nestles closer
smothering himself into growth, the river rises, my husband's breathing
slows. Then a small hand taps my chin, slides its fingers around
my bottom teeth pulling my head down so I can see
large brown eyes trying to figure out who I am.

Where I Don't Live

Tiny squares, triangles and hexagons
arranged in a window pane, illuminated
by the sun, a colorful flower pattern—
daisies, maybe lilies, maybe both.
The house is chocolate brown. It's not
the window where I watched lightning split a tree
or where a stranger watched me sleep.
Children crawl up the stairs, rainbow colors
highlight their bouncing hair,
memories they'll share with their children.
Outside, autumn leaves scattered at my feet,
as I push the stroller, turn to stone.
I stumble among their teetering under my weight.
The stroller wobbles left and right and back
until we turn towards home, his eyes still closed,
face relaxed so the lips are slightly parted,
leaves again falling. I walk slow.
The ground is smooth as I cross the bridge
stopping to listen for the water's surface, the way
it pushes around the rocks, always moving toward
something, but also moving away from where it's been.

Disconnected

The answering machine light remains solid,
the empty side of my bed is full
of new pillows. It is almost midnight
and I sit at the kitchen table folding
a math book closed, my homework
tucked between like a tongue
wilted against the lower lip. My son
has kicked off his sheet so I lift
his pillow-soft legs but as I cover him
he walks over the sheet, the slightest
touch draws this reaction.
I press my cheek against his forehead,
listen to his breath and kiss him. In the house
there is the dishwasher
and silence, two sounds that cradle me
through nights since his father
finally left. I circle through
rooms before bed and think of
school and work and preschool
and bills and cleaning and laundry.
When I hear a sound my ears perk
but it's never the phone, I turned that off
months ago after listening to his voice
follow me through the house, trying, with a mere
pause and shift in tone, to get back inside my heart.

Sunday Rain

Sitting here on top of this swollen swamp,
flash flooding unsettles the dirt, expands
roots of the maple underneath the foundation.
I'm in my Sunday best. If the day goes my way
I will not change from sleep to sleep.
I am ready for the morning dishes, the rinse and clang
as I load them in the washer, coffee stewing.
I never wear a Sunday hat and today
I don't go outside, instead I light candles
and brush the dogs. Across the yard, the willow tree,
where have its roots gone? To the coastal aquifer
or the main city water-line, its weeping tendrils extending
into the glass where my lips drink the rain? Ah,
the cool earth brings me the gospel of its sodden state.
I've dressed in honor of the sleeping child; he walks
down the hall and speaks to me. I sit so he can rest his head.

Pupa

I point at the spot where my son's heart beats
and say, "there,

I'm always right there." He's five and learning how
to take the idea of me with him. I know love does not keep

people from leaving, but I don't know what does,
so I don't know what else to say. He just stands and sheds tears

so I repeat, "I'm always right there." But instead of knowing
he crawls on my lap into the wrap of my arms, his head tucked

under my chin and with my whole body I hold on
while remaining fragile enough for him to break through.

Domestic Meditation

Dust settles on the teapot sticking to grease
from fried taco shells; my pores open
under the aroma rain of Wesson air.
I strain my knees to frayed fibers—
seconds stretch out from the Grandfather clock.

A fly meanders

as a shadow flashes against the white-washed ceiling
an insatiable cycle that circulates dust-bunnies
and flaked flesh; the silenced phone bulges
with its bell rattling tones that ring nowhere.

A fly meanders

while I wonder how Buddhist monks breathe
when they protest with the singe of flesh—
their strength propagating the air as sour ash rains
on to strained cheeks and burns scars into distant retinas.

A fly meanders

as seconds retract into the clock—
the keeper of minutes stolen today.
I bow my head to time
lift my knees, breathe
and stand to turn off the silenced bell.

Spring Cleaning in Winter

I help her throw away two-year-old sour cream,
the nearly empty cleaning products, two, three,
no, six bottles under the sink,
congealed drippings, scent of pine
and winter evening rain. Unopened
mail, paper clips, rubber bands; places to sit
dwindled among jackets, throw bags, outdated
coupons, a small unused photo album.
I step over cat toys, divvy out items
into various rooms, close
her bathroom door for another day.
This is not the first door I have closed,
there have been many—
the musty smell of youth
seeps through the cracks;
dirt and grime from skinned
knees on my bike, the wind I would ride
down the hill, a freedom
I wouldn't know what to do with,
what it meant. I close doors
to preserve, to know I can,
to know doors exist, that transition happens,
that it will happen to me.
I look at the bathroom door—
to me it is a portal, the only
place where I feel the tactile presence
of my body, the softening curves in my hips,
the marks where my son grew inside me.
I trace my calves and thighs,
the rough dry skin, the years of track,
of running in the dark, of becoming a woman.
I have no need to cover
the perishing of my body.
I open the door again,

look in the mirror as I did
fifteen years ago and reveal myself
through the pandemonium.
And this is where I want to be,
this place of knowing middle
age, not a thing of the future,
not a happening to someone else.
I see her through the doorway,
in the other room, the matted hair,
the bathrobe, the way she stuffs mail
in the over-stuffed holder;
I see her mornings in the piles
of towels on the linoleum.
It's what we do, watch a loved one
live in the luggage of their sadness.
I put another pill bottle in a basket
and close the door.

Shelter

Sometimes I don't know how to accept

your acceptance, so I want to leave
the keys to your house in a bus station

locker before buying a ticket.
You see, I am an immigrant

to living—divided between doing
and being—I kindle shelter

and emanate belief. So when I nestle
into you it is a coming to, a nook of solace.

Your rising chest stirs the only gust of wind.

In Parentheses

It's Saturday and we sit on the floor
piecing together Lego® houses and flying cars

and my five year old asks what's going to happen
after he dies. An old white man with a beard

emerges from the clouds of my imagination
with a few harps and our missing dog.

Brown eyes search my face for the safety of words.

It's Sunday and he's eleven. We sit at the kitchen table
finishing homework and he's instructed

to use a hyphen or parentheses in a sentence
while describing what he hopes to be true

in what he knows of religion. He begins with admitting
to no belief, and in parentheses (*but I hope*

there's an afterlife) states it is his preference over darkness.

To Have a House

Tape the door frame
careful to press edges

without a wrinkle
follow along the ceiling, floorboards

surround the window pane

watch the roller glide through
heavy smooth liquid

the first stroke on solid surface—a stripe

a white backdrop. What does it mean
to have a house in the world

to have it connect to poetry—
a white page ready

for the work of words across it—
the sublime falling to its graces?

What does it mean to shelter
a loved one? to allow for refuge?

A secret room
the proper color

for wiping tears on sheets.

History of Now

The inside of your house mimics
the growing night and candles

further melt the evening. We feed
off each other's eyes and leave

our bones of youth on the plate.
You flip a switch, mock daylight

and wash away our hunger. I dump scraps
into the trash. Midnight approaches.

Foundation

It took all my grandmother's strength
to open and close her curtains weighted

with polyester and years of *Price is Right*.
The seamless movement of dawn and dusk

filtered through the living room casting
shadows where I would sometimes sleep

under an orangesicle-colored afghan on the couch.
She played solitaire and ate homemade chicken soup.

I never heard the hum of her vacuum. There was time
to sit around the table eating salad out of a bowl while

dinner sat on a plate. The longest I ever lived
in one house was visits to my grandmother.

Barely an adult, I cared for her after bronchitis
flared the emphysema. She trailed a tube around

the house that attached her life to her breath,
floating, like in a dream, attached by the silver chord.

There was a science to divvying pills into their little boxes.
Every day of the week, every four hours per day. I would

do a few dishes, she would want to reheat soup, I would heat
some for us both while she rest in her chair, the oxygen machine

whirring her to sleep before I sat across the room on her couch,
both of us breathing and not breathing.

I am. I burn.

After a few sips
of single barrel bourbon
a howl releases, but I remain quiet
after midnight on my southern
suburban porch; the breeze tucks in the sleeping
pills of middle America. I'm reminded
of the first time I ate acid—
blood never looked so rich—like paint
it dripped slowly down my shin, like the beginning
of a Pollock mural, I too was *in* the painting, walking around,
letting it dry that way—I noticed how other people
sat quietly after dinner, florescent hues flashing
through parted sheer curtains; their eyes transfixed,
mouths pointing to the floor. I stood outside
my own house, blinds twisted tight, stove light unable
to peek through. Tonight, I don't watch people
through their window. Without opening my eyes I taste salt
pouring from their salt shaker. I see blood on the mattress.

You or I

We sit close on the couch swirling
2002 *Black Chicken* Zin

velvet petals, chocolate, black currant.
You feed me strawberries

lightly touch my arm. I look down
and for a moment do not know the age of us

and wonder who will die first—
do we choose someone to live with

or someone to watch us die
dump our bed pans, wash the creases

under our knees, the back of our neck?—
You lift my chin and lock our eyes.

Are you wondering if I would do that for you?

Visitors

Whether my stepfather is inside it, I don't know
but at any given moment his ailing body continues
to get up, searching for fire. At night rummaging wakes
us and we find him elbow deep in drawers, unlit cigarette
between his pink chapped lips. Mom offers a light
and leads him to the couch, petite arm around his shoulders.
The ember glows, his eyes shut tight against air.
She slides the cigarette out of his mouth and smokes it for him.

His brother welcomed me by pointing out the morphine
in the refrigerator, the list of phone numbers on a notepad,
the calendar with everyone's arrival and departure dates.
Now that I'm here he can stop chasing death wrapped
in his brother's body, guided by the tumor behind blue eyes.
I make a grocery list and plan a week's worth of dinners.

My aunt and uncle level their RV in the driveway
making it almost normal to stand in the kitchen
and wash dishes. After dinner, the desert sinks into darkness.
My aunt sweeps the already swept kitchen, the uncles' drink
at the table in silence and I flip pages in the recliner.
My stepfather is awake and propped up on the couch,
shoulders folded forward. Mom scratches his back
stares with his gaze at the TV. He turns his head, settles his eyes
on her as if for the first, middle, and last time. Smiles. Rubs her knee.
"What can I get you?" she says. He scans the room, pulls close
his empty hands, looks into her eyes. "You know you're my girl."
Then he leans closer, "Why are all these people here?"

Planning

We search for a planter that best displays
the geranium and plan for a place to hold
our secrets after death—marble, stone,
a plume of smoke that dances with twilight,
ashes, simply ashes. It's Saturday and it's Spring
so every bright flower wants to be tucked
into the beds of our yard, peaking azaleas
line the walkways where pale feet, having been hidden
all winter, glide through aisles of lilies,
petunias and creeping juniper. Fences align
in sheets from tall to short; white, steel and stained
mahogany red. We pause among the Dogwood saplings
and I tell you I love how their small white flowers sprinkle
over darkened limbs, that grow even darker as the flowers bloom.

A Way of Life

My mother remembers sitting in the shade
      on an over-sized porch during Arizona summers
        at the calloused leathery feet of her great-grandmother
—this is what I know of my native heritage except for the story
      of my great-great-great-grandfather who married
      a Blackfoot Indian from the high Dakotas.
A Scandinavian immigrant looking for home
      he flipped a coin: tails east, heads west.
      I was born in California without gold
rush in my blood, but a need to keep moving. My sister keeps a post office
      box so mail is unable to follow her home; my mom's sister,
      whom I never knew, committed suicide and my grandfather explained
she was born into the wrong life. My father must think
      he fathered the wrong family. He lives on a golf course in the city
      where I was born and like his father did to him he speaks to no one
but his new wife. And so this is what my son will know of his heritage:
      that moving is a way to find home, that those who stay
      might not want to be found, and that his cheekbones and skin tone
      connect to the deepest roots of his country.

To My Fiancé

We plan for unknowing, two blind
lovers in hope of connecting our present

tenderness with a future
but it is you who taught me forever

is a mere idea. Love is filling crosswords
by the bedside while listening for

steady breath to utter a hardened sigh
or an I'm thirsty so I can once again

show my love of your life
even if your life happens to be dying

and our love is left to float not
forever, but through the market

across balconies where
love-stricken stares won't notice it reach

the meadow in early fall where it rests
upon wilting grasses, snuggles deep

in the soil until it decomposes, love.
No longer identifiable it wafts sweetly

from petals of a wildflower giving
passersby reassurance of forever

but we know they only smell the moment
one more step and it's gone.

Born and raised in Northern California, **Cheryl Wilder** has made her home in North Carolina for the past twenty-three years. She holds degrees from the University of North Carolina at Wilmington and Vermont College of Fine Arts, where she earned her MFA in 2010. Her work has appeared in a number of journals, including *Cream City Review, Hunger Mountain, Literary Mama, Connotation Press,* and *Numéro Cinq.* Along with her husband, Cheryl owns a small web development company in the greater Triangle Area. When she's not the accountant, office manager or web marketing strategist, she works as content creator and web designer. She's the mother of three boys and the wife of one grateful man. You can find her at bornwilder.com.

www.ingramcontent.com/pod-product-compliance
Lightning Source LLC
LaVergne TN
LVHW021128080426
835510LV00021B/3360